EXPRESSWAY TO PERFECT CHINESE PRONUNCIATION

YILU ZHAO

EXPRESSWAY TO PERFECT CHINESE PRONUNCIATION

Second Edition

PEETERS
LEUVEN - PARIS - WALPOLE, MA
2012

D/2012/0602/123
ISBN 978-90-429-2716-2

内容简介

内容

三套语音练习和一个常见错误发音评述。练习及评述都配有录音。

特点

1 指出（母语为英语或荷兰语的）学生中常见的语音错误，使其能主动避免这些错误。
2 通过语音对比，提高正误音识别能力，以保发音准确。
3 以半三声作为三声的基调及练习重点，以便避免半三声过高的问题。
4 在初期反复用声调链（用四种声调连续念同一个音）进行练习。在练发音的同时，加深对声调的印象，以便能够以声调链为依据，找到所需声调的相对高度。
5 在朗读练习中，根据语音分类的练习在选词时尽量做到声调搭配多样化，以声调分类的练习在选词时尽量做到语音多样化。

第一套练习

用于零起点教学，包括听和读两种。
听力练习包括:
(1)辨别正误语音，(2)辨别正误声调。
朗读练习包括:
语音:(1)该单元新介绍的声韵母的练习，(2) 相似音的对比，如: zi-ze, zi-zhi。
声调:(1)单一声调的练习，(2)由四个基本声调(第三声为半三声)组成的声调链的练习，(3)不同声调搭配的练习。

第二套练习

是用于复习的朗读练习。
每个要练习的声、韵母出现于四个字或词(组)中: 1 单音节字，2 双音节的第一音节，3 双音节的第二音节，4 双音节的两个音节。
每一类别(声母、韵母、声调)的练习后部均有一个可用于测试的练习。每个练习由30个拼音词组成，其中包括所有的声、韵母和所有的声调搭配。
易掌握的声母m, f, n, l, h, y, w 没有专门练习。
儿化韵的练习根据儿化音的三种类别，由三组练习组成。
书后附有语音语调规则简要说明。

第三套练习

是前两套练习的补充:
1 与第一套练习中的听力练习内容与顺序相同，每课补充5个词，共10课。
2 与第二套练习中的朗读练习相似。每个要练习的声、韵母出现于10个词中，而且大部分在两个音节中都出现。

Preface

There are already many textbooks on Chinese pronunciation, why do I work on another one? In teaching Chinese pronunciation to foreign learners during the past 25 years, I noticed repeatedly the same types of mispronunciations, and I found that a major cause for learners who spoke Chinese with a foreign accent was not that they were unable to pronounce those sounds correctly, but that they were unaware of the nuances between correct and incorrect pronunciations. This is because generally speaking, people are less sensitive to nuances in unfamiliar sounds. Hence it is necessary to **point out these typical mispronunciations**, so that the learners can watch out and be their own teachers in trying to improve their pronunciation. In addition, it is more efficient to concentrate, in exercises, on sounds which are difficult for our (English/Dutch speaking) learners, rather than spending equal time on every sound. Thus this book came out. It was first published in 2000 with 2 sets of exercises and a discussion on common problems in pronunciation. Now supplementary exercises are added as the third set. To learners who do not have sufficient individual help from their teachers on their pronunciation, yet who want to speak Chinese with perfect pronunciation, this book will be particularly useful.

Although in textbooks the full contour of the third tone has always been introduced as the norm of the third tone, with the half third tone as its variation, in this book **the half third tone is taken as the norm.** This is because when one is used to the slightly rising end of the full third tone, it is difficult for him to cut its rising end to have the half third tone. Consequentially his intended half third tone often sounds like second tone. Since it is difficult to change a habit and in reality the half third tone is much more frequently used than the full third tone, in this book the half third tone is taken as the norm.

Descriptions of how to pronounce sounds in Chinese, which can be found in many textbooks of Chinese, are omitted here. This book consists of **a discussion about mispronunciations** frequently found in Dutch or English speaking learners and **3 sets of exercises**: one for introducing the sounds, one for reviewing and the third as supplementary to the first two. In listening exercises correct and wrong pronunciations are compared.

The signs of *pinyin* are used in descriptions of sounds most of the time. The signs of the phonetic transcription and linguistic terms, which are unfamiliar to most learners, are rarely used. The phonetic signs used here are put into square brackets, while the signs of *pinyin* used in the discussion are put in italics, e.g. [ji], *yi*.

Set One

This set of exercises, which can be used to get acquainted with the pronunciation and tones in Chinese, is made up of two kinds of exercises: (1) **reading exercises**, which **focus on difficult sounds, with contrasting sounds in pairs**; and (2) **listening exercises, for sound or tone discrimination**.

In exercise (B) of units 1- 4 the four basic tones are practiced in a string of four syllables, e.g. *mī-mí-mǐ-mì,* to make the learners perceive the tones not only with their respective features, but also in relation to each other. Moreover, the repetition of this string engraves on the learners' mind a framework of the tones, which can serve as a tone indicator when they try to produce a given tone.

The listening exercises are of two kinds: exercise (A) focuses on the pronunciation, and exercise (B) focuses on the tones. In these exercises the learners are asked to identify, from the three readings of the same sound, the correct one(s).

Set Two

This set, in which **all exercises are grouped on the basis of the features of the sounds or of the tones**, can be used as a systematic review of the difficult sounds and tones of *pinyin,* as well as exercises to be selected in relation to given problems. For instance, those who have difficulty with '*j, q, x*' sounds can concentrate on exercises of this group, while those who have difficulty with the half third tone can pick out the exercises of the third tone combinations.

In all exercises attention has been paid to ensure that in each group of words there is variation not only in the initials or/and the finals, but also in tone combination patterns. The initials which hardly cause problems - *m, f, n, l, h, y, w* - are not taken as target sounds in the exercises.

The suffix '*er*', which is pronounced in different ways according to the final to which it is affixed, is introduced in 3 groups of exercises, on the basis of the ways in which it is pronounced: (1) simple combination, (2) modified combination, and (3) mergence, in which the *e* sound in *er* is absent.

There are 3 general exercises of 30 words which include all initials, all finals and all basic tone combination patterns of pinyin. These exercises can also be used as tests of pronunciation and tones of Chinese. At the end of this set, there is an exercise of sentences with words either of the same tone, or with the neutral tone and the suffix *er*.

Set Three

This set of supplementary exercises also consists of 2 types: (1) **Listening exercises**, which are similar to those in Set One. There are 10 units, which correspond to the units in Set one. In each unit there are 5 words. (2) **Reading exercises**, with target sounds identical to the ones taken in Set Two. There are 10 words for each target sound, which in most cases is found in both syllables. Efforts are made to avoid, as much as possible, repetition of the tone patterns among those 10 words. In addition there are also separate exercises for the 2 types of the final -*i*: the finals of *zi* and *zhi,* and exercises of 3 pairs of contrasting sounds: -*i*1 vs. –*i*2, *i* vs. –*i*, and *u* vs. *ü*.

Yilu Zhao
University of Leuven, Belgium

TABLE OF CONTENTS

Content **Page**

Set Three: Supplementary exercises

Discussion of Common Problems in Pronunciation and Tones

SET ONE

The possible combinations of an initial and a final, which are to be read, are marked with the sign '+' in the exercises, though in some cases a given tone of such a combination does not exist in real usage. In the listening exercises of sound and tone discrimination, each word is read 3 times. Those which are read correctly should be identified. The keys to the listening exercises can be found at the end of the book.

Unit 1

Initials: m f n l h
Finals: a i ao
Tones: all tones

(1) Reading exercises

(A)

	ā	á	ǎ	ǎ[1]	à	a
m	+	+	+	+	+	+
f	+	+	+	+	+	+
n	+	+	+	+	+	+
l	+	+	+	+	+	+
h	+	+	+	+	+	+

(B)

	ī - í - ǐ - ì				āo-áo-ǎo-ào			
m	+	+	+	+	+	+	+	+
f								
n	+	+	+	+	+	+	+	+
l	+	+	+	+	+	+	+	+
h					+	+	+	+

(2) Listening exercises

(A) Identify words read with correct pronunciations

1. fā, A B C; 2. mì, A B C; 3. hǎo, A B C; 4. lí, A B C; 5. nào, A B C.

(B) Identify words read with correct tones

1. fā, A B C; 2. mì, A B C; 3. hǎo, A B C; 4. lí, A B C; 5. nào, A B C.

[1] The first ǎ in exercise (A) is read with the half third tone, and the second with the full contour of the third tone.

Unit 2

Initials: y w
Finals: o u ü e en ie
Tone: first tone

(1) Reading exercises

(A)

	ō	ū	ǖ	ē	ēn	iē
y			+			+
w	+	+			+	
m	+	+			+	+
f	+	+			+	
n		+	+	+	+	+
l		+	+	+		+
h		+		+	+	

(B)

	ō - ó - ǒ - ò	ē - é - ě - è	ēn-én-ěn-èn	iē - ié - iě - iè
y				+ + + +
w	+ + + +		+ + + +	
m	+ + + +		+ + + +	+ + + +
f	+ + + +		+ + + +	
n		+ + + +	+ + + +	+ + + +
l		+ + + +		+ + + +
h		+ + + +	+ + + +	

(2) Listening exercises

(A) Identify words read with correct pronunciations

1. yū, A B C; 2. yē, A B C; 3. wō, A B C; 4. wū, A B C; 5. hē, A B C;
6. fēn, A B C; 7. niē, A B C; 8. mó, A B C; 9. lǚ, A B C; 10. mèn, A B C.

(B) Identify words read with correct tones

1. yū, A B C; 2. yē, A B C; 3. wō, A B C; 4. wū, A B C; 5. hē, A B C;
6. fēn, A B C; 7. niē, A B C; 8. mó, A B C; 9. lǚ, A B C; 10. mèn, A B C.

Unit 3

Initials: b d g, p t k
Tone: second tone

(1) Reading exercises

(A)

	á	í	ó	ú	é	áo	én	ié
b	+	+	+	+		+	+	+
p	+	+	+	+		+	+	+
d	+	+		+	+	+		+
t	+	+		+	+	+		+
g	+			+	+	+	+	
k	+			+	+	+	+	

(B)

	āo-áo-ǎo-ào				ēn-én-ěn-èn				iē-ié-iě-iè			
b	+	+	+	+	+	+	+	+	+	+	+	+
p	+	+	+	+	+	+	+	+	+	+	+	+
d	+	+	+	+					+	+	+	+
t	+	+	+	+					+	+	+	+
g	+	+	+	+	+	+	+	+				
k	+	+	+	+	+	+	+	+				

(C)
bá pá, bí pí, bó pó, bú pú, báo páo, bén pén, bié pié
dá tá, dí tí, dú tú, dé té, dáo táo, dié tié
gá ká, gú kú, gé ké, gáo káo, gén kén
gǔbō pà bú pà tā bàba?
tā bú pà tā bàba,
tā bàba pà tā.

(2) Listening exercises

(A) Identify words read with correct pronunciations

1. bó, A B C; 2. pén, A B C; 3. dié, A B C; 4. tú, A B C; 5. ké, A B C; 6. píbāo, A B C; 7. géhé, A B C; 8. táopǎo, A B C; 9. túdì, A B C; 10. pípa, A B C.

(B) Identify words read with correct tones
1. bó, A B C; 2. pén, A B C; 3. dié, A B C; 4. tú, A B C; 5. ké, A B C; 6. píbāo, A B C; 7. géhé, A B C; 8. táopǎo, A B C; 9. túdì, A B C; 10. pípa, A B C.

Unit 4

Initials: zh ch sh r, z c s
Final: -i
Tone: half third tone

(1) Reading exercises

(A)

	ǐ	ǎ	ǎo	ǔ	ěn
zh	+	+	+	+	+
ch	+	+	+	+	+
sh	+	+	+	+	+
r	+		+	+	+
z	+	+	+	+	+
c	+	+	+	+	+
s	+	+	+	+	+

(B)

	ī -	í -	ǐ -	ì	ē -	é -	ě -	è
zh	+	+	+	+	+	+	+	+
ch	+	+	+	+	+	+	+	+
sh	+	+	+	+	+	+	+	+
r	+	+	+	+	+	+	+	+
z	+	+	+	+	+	+	+	+
c	+	+	+	+	+	+	+	+
s	+	+	+	+	+	+	+	+

(C)
zhī zhē, chī chē, shī shē, rī rē
zī zē, cī cē, sī sē

zī zhī, cī chī, sī shī
zē zhē, cē chē, sē shē

bǐzhí, tǐzhì, cǐshí, zhǐshì, sǐshī
lǐzhì, chǐzi, bǐshì, shǐshī, zǐdì

(2) Listening exercises

(A) Identify words read with correct pronunciations
1. sǐ, A B C; 2. cǐ, A B C; 3. shǐ, A B C; 4. zhǐ, A B C; 5. chǐ, A B C; 6. zǐsè, A B C; 7. shǐshū, A B C; 8. dǐzhì, Λ B C; 9. zhǐzé, A B C; 10. rìzi, A B C.

(B) Identify words read with correct tones
1. sǐ, A B C; 2. cǐ, A B C; 3. shǐ, A B C; 4. zhǐ, A B C; 5. chǐ, A B C; 6. zǐsè, A B C; 7. shǐshū, A B C; 8. dǐzhì, A B C; 9. zhǐzé, A B C; 10. rìzi, A B C.

Unit 5

Finals: ai ei an ang eng ou ong
Tone: full contour of the third tone and third tone changes into the second tone

(1) Reading exercises

(A)

	ǎi	ěi	ǎn	ǎng	ěng	ǒu	ǒng
zh	+	+	+	+	+	+	+
ch	+		+	+	+	+	+
sh	+	+	+	+	+	+	
r			+	+	+	+	+
z	+	+	+	+	+	+	+
c	+		+	+	+	+	+
s	+		+	+	+	+	+

(B)
zǎn zǎng, zěn zěng, zǎn zěn, zǎng zěng
zhǎn zhǎng, zhěn zhěng, zhǎn zhěn, zhǎng zhěng

bǎi běi, pǎi pěi, bǎi pǎi, běi pěi
dǎo dǒu, tǎo tǒu, dǎo tǎo, dǒu tǒu

(C)
nǐhǎo, kěyǐ, bǐcǐ, yǔfǎ, yǒnggǎn
yě hěn hǎo, wǒ yě yǒu, wǒ zhǎo nǐ
wǒ gěi nǐ mǎi bǐ, wǒ zhǐ yǒu wǔběn

(2) Listening exercises

(A) Identify words read with correct pronunciations
1. zǒu, A B C; 2. pěng, A B C; 3. dǎn, A B C; 4. tǎng, A B C;
5. hǎigǎng, A B C; 6. shěngwěi, A B C; 7. chǎngzhǎng, A B C;
8. zǒngtǒng, A B C; 9. lǎobǎn, A B C; 10. shǐzhě, A B C.

(B) Identify words read with correct tones
1. zǒu, A B C; 2. pěng, A B C; 3. dǎn, A B C; 4. tǎng, A B C;
5. hǎigǎng, A B C; 6. shěngwěi, A B C; 7. chǎngzhǎng, A B C;
8. zǒngtǒng, A B C; 9. lǎobǎn, A B C; 10. shǐzhě, A B C.

Unit 6

Initials: j q x
Finals: in ing
Tone: fourth tone

(1) Reading exercises

(A)

	ì	ìn	ìng
j	+	+	+
q	+	+	+
x	+	+	+

(B)
jìjū, jìjú, jìjǔ, jìjù
qìqū, qìqú, qìqǔ, qìqù
xìxū, xìxú, xìxǔ, xìxù
jìnjìng, qìnqìng, xìnxìng

(C)
jīdòng, xìnrèn, jìngrán, sòngxìn, jìxing
qíngxing, jìnqíng, jìnxíng, xìngqíng, qǐngjìn
qīngjìng, xìnxī, qíngxù, jìxù, chóngqìng

(2) Listening exercises

(A) Identify words read with correct pronunciations
1. xù, A B C; 2. jì, A B C; 3. qìn, A B C; 4. xìn, A B C; 5. jìnqū, A B C; 6. xìngqu, A B C; 7. qíngxù, A B C; 8. qìngxìng, A B C; 9. jùjí, A B C; 10. jīqì, A B C.

(B) Identify words read with correct tones
1. xù, A B C; 2. jì, A B C; 3. qìn, A B C; 4. xìn, A B C; 5. jìnqū, A B C; 6. xìngqu, A B C; 7. qíngxù, A B C; 8. qìngxìng, A B C; 9. jùjí, A B C; 10. jīqì, A B C.

Unit 7

Finals: ia iao ian iang iu iong
Tone: neutral tone

(1) Reading exercises

(A) (Exercise (A) in units 7-9 do not have tone marks in the text. The first tone will be used in the recording, but one may also use another tone.)

	i	ia	iao	ian	iang	iu	iong	in	ing	ie
j	+	+	+	+	+	+	+	+	+	+
q	+	+	+	+	+	+	+	+	+	+
x	+	+	+	+	+	+	+	+	+	+

(B)
píjiǔ, pínqióng, zhàoxiàng, jiǒngjìng, xīngjiàn
jīxiào, xíngxiōng, qǐngqiú, qiǎngjiù, jiānqiáng
jiānzi, qiánzi, jiǎozi, xiùzi, qiǎzi
jiāngjiu, qiángshang, xiǎnbai, jiàqian, xiùqi

(C)
māma, yéye, nǎinai, jiùjiu
xiānsheng, qiáojian, jiǎngjiu, xiàngsheng
zhǐzhe, xiǎngguo, jiǎnzi, jiǔge
qǐngba, rěnzhe, zǒngde, sǐle
xǐxǐ, zǒuzǒu, zhǎozhǎo, xiěxiě[2]
xiǎojiě, nǐ hǎohǎo xiǎngxiǎng ba.

(2) Listening exercises

(A) Identify words read with correct pronunciations
1. jiā, A B C; 2. qiǎo, A B C; 3. qióng, A B C; 4. xiù, A B C;
5. xiōngqiāng, A B C; 6. jiēqià, A B C; 7. xiàqu, A B C;
8. xiānliang, A B C; 9. xiōngdi, A B C; 10. jiùying, A B C.

(B) Identify words read with correct tones
1. jiā, A B C; 2. qiǎo, A B C; 3. qióng, A B C; 4. xiù, A B C;
5. xiōngqiāng, A B C; 6. jiēqià, A B C; 7. xiàqu, A B C;
8. xiānliang, A B C; 9. xiōngdi, A B C; 10. jiùying, A B C.

[2] Those 4 words are verbs. Rules of tone sandhi for reduplicated third tone words: 1) verbs: 33 becomes 20, e.g. those 4 words; 2) nouns: 33 becomes 30, e.g. nǎinǎi, jiějiě; 3) adverbs: 33 becomes 31, e.g. hǎohǎo, yuǎnyuǎnde. See also the discussion part and end note nr. 3.

Unit 8

Finals: ua uo uai ui uan un uang

(1) Reading exercises

(A)

	ua	uo	uai	ui	uan	un	uang
zh	+	+	+	+	+	+	+
ch		+	+	+	+	+	+
sh	+	+	+	+	+	+	+
r		+		+	+	+	
z		+		+	+	+	
c		+		+	+	+	
s		+		+	+	+	

(B)
suǒyǒu, shuāihuǐ, huáchuán, guǎngkuò, kùnhuò
huǒtuǐ, zhuǎnwān, cūnzhuāng, kōusuo, huìhuà

(C)
bā bā, bā bá, bā bǎ, bā bà, bā ba
bá bā, bá bá, bá bǎ, bá bà, bá ba
bǎ bā, bǎ bá, bǎ bǎ, bǎ bà, bǎ ba
bà bā, bà bá, bà bǎ, bà bà, bà ba

(2) Listening exercises

(A) Identify words read with correct pronunciations
1. zhuā, A B C; 2. zuò, A B C; 3. guǎi, A B C; 4. kuí, A B C;
5. huánghūn, A B C; 6. zuǒyòu, A B C; 7. zuìkuài, A B C;
8. guóhuà, A B C; 9. cúnkuǎn, A B C; 10. guòguān, A B C.

(B) Identify words read with correct tones
1. zhuā, A B C; 2. zuò, A B C; 3. guǎi, A B C; 4. kuí, A B C;
5. huánghūn, A B C; 6. zuǒyòu, A B C; 7. zuìkuài, A B C;
8. guóhuà, A B C; 9. cúnkuǎn, A B C; 10. guòguān, A B C.

Unit 9

Finals: üe üan ün

(1) Reading exercises

(A)

	ü	üe	üan	ün		ü	üe	üan	ün
j	+	+	+	+	n	+	+		
q	+	+	+	+	l	+	+		
x	+	+	+	+					

(B)
xuèyuán, qúnjū, xuéxiào, xuējiǎn, jùjí
quànjià, juéxīn, quézi, juānqián, quánjú
juānxiàn, xūnjué, jìxù, juéjiàng, rénqún

(C)
chūqu, lùxù, fùnǚ, xuānchuán, gùjū
lùqǔ, guànjūn, húxū, quánbù, zhǔnquè
fùyu, jūnguān, zǔqǔ, chūnxùn, quántuán

(2) Listening exercises

(A) Identify words read with correct pronunciations
1. qún, A B C; 2. xuān, A B C; 3. xuè, A B C; 4. juǎn, A B C; 5. chǔxù, A B C; 6. chuánxùn, A B C; 7. quánsù, A B C; 8. zūnxún, A B C; 9. quèqiè, A B C; 10. quēxiàn, A B C.

(B) Identify words read with correct tones
1. qún, A B C; 2. xuān, A B C; 3. xuè, A B C; 4. juǎn, A B C; 5. chǔxù, A B C; 6. chuánxùn, A B C; 7. quánsù, A B C; 8. zūnxún, A B C; 9. quèqiè, A B C; 10. quēxiàn, A B C.

Unit 10

Final: er

(1) Reading exercises

(A)[ər]: 2nd or 3rd tone
érqiě, xìng'ér, érzi, ěrduo, értóng
mùěr, yòuěr, rán'ér, shíér, yīng'ér

(B)[ar]: 4th tone
shíèr, dìèr, èrbǎi, èrqiān, èrwàn

(2) Listening exercises

(A) Identify words read with correct pronunciations
1. érqiě, A B C; 2. èrbǎi, A B C; 3. ěrduo, A B C;
4. shíèr, A B C; 5. yīng'ér, A B C.

(B) Identify words read with correct tones
1. érqiě, A B C; 2. èrbǎi, A B C; 3. ěrduo, A B C;
4. shíèr, A B C; 5. yīng'ér, A B C.

SET TWO

I. Pronunciation

1. Initials

1.1. b d g p t k

b — A. bù, B. bōli, C. huǒbàn, D. bīngbáo.
p — A. pù, B. pàomò, C. chúnpǔ, D. pēngpài.
d — A. dù, B. dāngrán, C. jiǎodù, D. dǎdǔ.
t — A. tù, B. tánhuà, C. shuǐtǒng, D. tiāotì.
g — A. gù, B. gānjìng, C. déguó, D. gǒnggù.
k — A. kù, B. kāfēi, C. xīnkǔ, D. kǎnkě.

1.2. z c s zh ch sh r

z — A. zāng, B. zǎocāo, C. chēngzàn, D. zāizāng.
c — A. cāng, B. cānjiā, C. zhùcè, D. cǎocóng.
s — A. sāng, B. suíbiàn, C. yǔsǎn, D. sùsòng.
zh — A. zhāng, B. zhǔnbèi, C. xúnzhǎo, D. zhùzhái.
ch — A. chāng, B. chǎnshēng, C. zuǐchún, D. chóuchàng.
sh — A. shāng, B. shǔyú, C. chènshān, D. shénshèng.
r — A. rāng, B. rènshi, C. dǎrǎo, D. réngrán.

1.3. j q x

j — A. jiān, B. jiǎzhuāng, C. gǎnjué, D. jīngjì.
q — A. qiān, B. quánshuǐ, C. shēnqǐng, D. qīnqiè.
x — A. xiān, B. xǐhuan, C. zhāoxiá, D. xīnxuè.

1.4. General exercise of the initials

(1) pāoqì, (2) lìnsè, (3) jiǎnglì, (4) xīujià, (5) xiōnghuái, (6) dúlà, (7) gǎnqiǎo, (8) cāiquán, (9) xìng'ér, (10) júzi, (11) kuīsǔn, (12) péngzhàng, (13) wěiba, (14) xièxie, (15) huǒji, (16) lìshǐ, (17) sōusuǒ, (18) jǐnzhāng, (19) cháonòng, (20) mángrán, (21) gēzi, (22) qìyuē, (23) xùnfú, (24) táidēng, (25) xuánzhuǎn, (26) qiǎnbó, (27) huàzhuāng, (28) tiáojié, (29) hūnyīn, (30) shènzhì.

2. Finals

2.1. a o e i -i u ü

a — A. là, B. mǎshàng, C. bàodá, D. dàmā.
o — A. mò, B. mófàn, C. huópo, D. wòfó.
e — A. lè, B. shèyǐng, C. qìchē, D. hégé.
i — A. lì, B. mǐfàn, C. fēijī, D. lìqi.
-i1 — A. zì, B. cīxiá, C. cánsī, D. zǐsì.
-i2 — A. shì, B. rìqī, C. dàshǐ, D. zhīchí.
u — A. lù, B. gūniang, C. shāngǔ, D. hútu.
ü — A. lǜ, B. jūliú, C. dìqū, D. xùqǔ.

2.2. ai ei ao ou an en ang eng ong

ai — A. zāi, B. mǎishū, C. huógāi, D. báicài.
ei — A. zéi, B. bèizi, C. yīnwèi, D. gěishéi.
ao — A. zǎo, B. shāobing, C. chídào, D. sāorǎo.
ou — A. zǒu, B. lóutī, C. hēzhōu, D. shòuròu.
an — A. zǎn, B. fánnǎo, C. shàngbān, D. nánkàn.
en — A. zěn, B. běnlái, C. xiàchén, D. rènzhēn.
ang — A. zāng, B. hángxíng, C. xīzàng, D. shāngchǎng.
eng — A. zèng, B. réngjiù, C. xīnténg, D. lěngfēng.
ong — A. zǒng, B. chōngpèi, C. yóuyǒng, D. gòngtóng.

2.3. ia iao ian iang ie iu in ing iong

ia — A. qiǎ, B. jiǎshè, C. hǎixiá, D. qiājià.
iao — A. qiǎo, B. biāozhì, C. shuìjiào, D. xiǎoqiáo.
ian — A. qián, B. jiānchí, C. wēixiǎn, D. diànxiàn.
iang — A. qiāng, B. jiǎnglì, C. jíxiáng, D. liàngqiàng.
ie — A. qiē, B. tiělù, C. xiāomiè, D. jièxié.
iu — A. qiū, B. niútuǐ, C. hējiǔ, D. xiùqiú.
in — A. qīn, B. mǐnjié, C. rénmín, D. qīnjìn.
ing — A. qǐng, B. píngzi, C. yǐjīng, D. xìngmíng.
iong — A. qióng, B. jiǒngpò, C. yīngxióng, D. xióngxióng.

2.4. ua uo uai ui uan un uang

ua — A. guā, B. kuākǒu, C. shuōhuà, D. shuǎhuá.
uo — A. guó, B. suǒqǔ, C. hěnduō, D. shuōcuò.
uai — A. guāi, B. huáiyí, C. qíguài, D. shuāihuài.
ui — A. guì, B. tuìxiū, C. gēnsuí, D. zuìguǐ.
uan — A. guān, B. ruǎnruò, C. lúnchuán, D. huànsuàn.
un — A. gùn, B. zūnshǒu, C. yúchǔn, D. húntún.
uang — A. guǎng, B. huǎnghuà, C. xiàshuāng, D. chuángkuàng.

2.5. üe üan ün

üe — A. jué, B. quézi, C. cèlüè, D. quēxuè.
üan — A. juān, B. xuǎnzé, C. bàoyuàn, D. yuánquán.
ün — A. jùn, B. yǔnxǔ, C. zīxún, D. jūnxùn.

2.6. er

2.6.1. The final er

er1 — A. ér, B. érqiě, C. ǒuěr, D. ěrduo.
er2 — A. èr, B. èrshí, C. shíèr, D. èrshíèr.

2.6.2. The suffix er

The words in this exercise, which are written without er, are read first without er, then with er.

(1) F + er (combination of the final and *er*)

a — A. làbā, B. dāobà, C. yìdá.
ia — A. rénjiā, B. yàojià, C. yìxiá.
ua — A. xiāngguā, B. huàhuà, C. jīzhuǎ.
i — A. fěnpí, B. xiǎomǐ, C. xiǎojī.
-i — A. guǒzhī, B. táicí, C. xiězì.
ü — A. jīnyú, B. mǎjū, C. xiǎoqǔ.
ie — A. táijiē, B. xiǎoxié, C. yìpiě.
üe — A. mùjué, B. yuèyuè, C. zhǔjué.

(2) F' + er (combination of the modified final and *er*)

(a) The 'n' at the end of the final is dropped:

en — e: A. cǎogēn, B. dàmén, C. yìběn.
an — a: A. hǎowán, B. mùbǎn, C. pòlàn.
ian — ia: A. huābiān, B. màipiàn, C. yìdiǎn.
uan — ua: A. yíchuàn, B. fànguǎn, C. dāngguān.
üan — üa: A. yuánquān, B. kǎojuàn, C. gōngyuán.
in — i: A. chōujīn, B. shāoxìn, C. jiǎoyìn.
un — u: A. duàndùn, B. méizhǔn, C. guānggùn.
ün — ü: A. héqún.

(b) The 'i' at the end of the final is dropped:

ei — e: A. mōhēi, B. yǎnlèi, C. xiǎozìbèi.
ai — a: A. mùsāi, B. xiǎohái, C. pínggài.
uai — ua: A. guāiguāi, B. yíkuài, C. mùkuài.
ui — u: A. yìduī, B. xiǎotuǐ, C. yíhuì.

(3) Fr (merging of the retroflex 'r' into the final)

u — A. xiǎozhū, B. xiǎolù, C. cháhú.
e — A. chànggē, B. xiǎohé, C. mótè.
o — A. niǎowō, B. fěnmò, C. méipó.
uo — A. xiǎoshuō, B. méicuò, C. yìduǒ.
ou — A. xiǎotōu, B. píhóu, C. nènròu.
iu — A. shuǐnīu, B. xiǎoqiú, C. yíliù.
ao — A. xiǎomāo, B. xiǎozào, C. máotáo.
iao — A. yúpiāo, B. qǔdiào, C. xiǎoniǎo.

ang — A. liútāng, B. guāráng, C. huàgàng.
iang — A. jǐxiāng, B. méiliàng, C. tǔqiáng.
uang — A. jièguāng, B. dànhuáng, C. yìhuǎng.
eng — A. xiǎofēng, B. tiàoshéng, C. ménfèng.
ing — A. xiǎobīng, B. cùpíng, C. suānxìng.
ong — A. nàozhōng, B. yǒukòng, C. xiǎochóng.
iong — A. xiǎoxióng.

(4) General exercise of the suffix er

(1) méihuā, (2) xiédài, (3) tǔsī, (4) yětù, (5) mìguàn, (6) jǐxià, (7) shǒujuàn, (8) bīngkuài, (9) xiǎocōng, (10) tóngqián, (11) kāimén, (12) rénqíng, (13) dǎgǔn, (14) yìdié, (15) bèiké, (16) lùkǒu, (17) zhǎoshì, (18) màisuì, (19) zhuājiū, (20) tǔkēng.

2.7. General exercise of the finals

(1) bākuài, (2) fǎnle, (3) qùchu, (4) pópo, (5) chìzé, (6) zhéchǐ, (7) zǎozǒu, (8) sǎnzhuāng, (9) shàngchuán, (10) néngrén, (11) hóngdēng, (12) zǎoxiá, (13) xuéyè, (14) jiānqiáng, (15) yǐngyìn, (16) xíngxiōng, (17) jiǎojié, (18) zuìguo, (19) wēncún, (20) guāngguāng, (21) yīngjùn, (22) xiūxi, (23) quèqiè, (24) shòuruò, (25) èrbǎi, (26) zuòchē, (27) értóng, (28) huājuǎnr, (29) qízǐr, (30) méishìr.

II. Tones

1. First tone

1&1: A. fēijī, B. cānjiā, C. ānxīn, D. biāoqiān.
1&2: A. bāngmáng, B. fēichuán, C. tūrán, D. jīngqí.
1&3: A. bēnpǎo, B. suānzǎor, C. qīngxǐng, D. jīnglǐ.
1&4: A. fēnbù, B. jīngguò, C. jiēqià, D. chēliàng.
2&1: A. tántiān, B. áozhōu, C. míngxīng, D. ránshāo.
3&1: A. huǒchē, B. hǎotīng, C. dǎkāi, D. shuǐxiāng.
4&1: A. qìchē, B. kuàngshān, C. rèxīn, D. zhànzhēng.

2. Second tone

2&1: A. huíjiā, B. júzhī, C. táidēng, D. chuángdān.
2&2: A. yóuqí, B. chángchéng, C. liánmáng, D. xuéxí.
2&3: A. quántǐ, B. méiyǒu, C. hélǐ, D. cóngcǐ.
2&4: A. zázhì, B. huíyì, C. hútòng, D. nánshòu.
1&2: A. hūrán, B. qīngnián, C. gōngyuán, D. kāimén.
3&2: A. yǔyán, B. yǎnyuán, C. kǒuhóng, D. yǐqián.
4&2: A. bàomíng, B. sìshí, C. guìtái, D. yuèqiú.

3. Third tone

3&1: A. kǒnghuāng, B. zǎocāo, C. xuěqiāo, D. chǎnshēng.
3&2: A. rǒngcháng, B. huǒtóng, C. nuǎnfáng, D. shuǐqú.
3&3: A. xuǎnjǔ, B. dǎoyǔ, C. biǎoyǎn, D. shuǐniǎo.
3&4: A. jǐngsè, B. chǎojià, C. xǐngmù, D. zǒulù.
1&3: A. suānnǎi, B. fāngfǎ, C. chōngjǐng, D. kāishǐ.
2&3: A. húběi, B. xióngwěi, C. míyǔ, D. qióngkǔ.
4&3: A. fùmǔ, B. xiàochuǎn, C. kàngtǐ, D. huìzhěn.

4. Fourth tone

4&1: A. jiànkāng, B. diàndēng, C. wèisuō, D. chènjī.
4&2: A. xìngmíng, B. xiàoróng, C. tuìpéi, D. mànyán.
4&3: A. chèdǐ, B. tiàoyuǎn, C. jùběn, D. fèipǐn.
4&4: A. shuìjiào, B. suìyuè, C. tuòyè, D. pànwàng.
1&4: A. biāozhì, B. xuānshì, C. yījù, D. xiānjìn.
2&4: A. túxiàng, B. wénhuà, C. xiángxì, D. wánjù.
3&4: A. sǔnhuài, B. yǎngqì, C. bǎngyàng, D. zhǐkòng.

5. Neutral tone

1&0: A. chība, B. qīngchu, C. gēge, D. zhēnde.
2&0: A. láiba, B. xuéguo, C. qiánbianr, D. shéide.

3&0: A. děngzhe, B. wǎnle, C. yǐzi, D. lǐtou.
4&0: A. zhàngfu, B. hùshi, C. làngtou, D. yuèliang.

III. General exercises

1. Words

(1) piāobó, (2) tǎndàng, (3) gǎikǒu, (4) jǐzi, (5) cāiquán, (6) xīnsi, (7) zànzhù, (8) chǎocài, (9) sìshī, (10) rénshēn, (11) tuìxiū, (12) yǒnghéng, (13) bǎituō, (14) názhe, (15) kǒngbù, (16) pēngrèn, (17) huányuán, (18) qióngkùn, (19) jiāqiáng, (20) ěrguāng, (21) juédìng, (22) lièchē, (23) fèiwu, (24) kuàihuó, (25) guāfēn, (26) zūnshǒu, (27) miànjin, (28) qúndǎo, (29) jùyǒu, (30) xiǎoháir.

2. Sentences

(1) jīntiān zhāngchūnshēng jiāo jiāngqīngxīn kāi fēijī.
today (name) teach (name) fly airplane
'Today Zhang Chunsheng teaches Jiang Qingxin to pilot an airplane.'

(2) yángqíngwén míngnián hái néng lái déguó xuéxí.
(name) next year still can come Germany study
'Next year Yang Qingwen can still come to Germany to study.'

(3) wǒ hěn xiǎng qǐng dǒngxiǎojiě gěi wǒ jiǎngjiǎng fǎyǔ yǔfǎ.
I very want ask (name) miss for I explain French grammar
'I want very much to ask Miss Dong to explain to me French grammar.'

(4) sòngzìzhì guòqù jiù zhù zài jiànzhù xì de sùshè.
(name) previously just live in architecture dept. P[3] dormitory
'Previously Song Zizhi lived in the dormitory of the Department of Architecture.'

(5) sūn xiānsheng, jīnr wǎnshang nín yǒukòngr ma?
(name) mister today evening you be free P
'Mr. Song, are you free this evening?'

[3] "P" stands for "Particle.

SET THREE SUPPLEMENTARY EXERCISES

Part One: Listening exercises

Each word will be, **first of all, read correctly once,** and then read 3 times, in which the number of correct ones could be 0-2.
Identify the words which are read correctly.

Unit 1
1. māomī, A B C; 2. máofà, A B C; 3. fāmá, A B C;
4. hǎola, A B C; 5. lìfǎ, A B C.

Unit 2
1. yèli, A B C; 2. wūmiè, A B C; 3. móhé, A B C;
4. yùmèn, A B C; 5. wǒè, A B C.

Unit 3
1. tiěké, A B C; 2. bēnbō, A B C; 3. pǎobù, A B C;
4. dàgē, A B C; 5. gūpì, A B C.

Unit 4
1. sìchǐ, A B C; 2. zīshì, A B C; 3. cǐzhì, A B C;
4. zhírì, A B C; 5. chìzì, A B C.

Unit 5
1. kǒubēi, A B C; 2. chéngzhǎng, A B C; 3. zàntóng, A B C;
4. shèngcài, A B C; 5. zhōngbān, A B C.

Unit 6
1. jīzhì, A B C; 2. cíqì, A B C; 3. xǐshì, A B C;
4. jìngxīn, A B C; 5. qīnqíng, A B C.

Unit 7
1. jiāojiē, A B C; 2. qiānqiǎng, A B C; 3. jiǔjiā, A B C;
4. xióngxìng, A B C; 5. qiǎngxiǎn, A B C.

Unit 8
1. zhuāngsuàn, A B C; 2. zuǐchún, A B C; 3. huāhuán, A B C;
4. guàizuì, A B C; 5. cúnhuó, A B C.

Unit 9
1. juānkuǎn, A B C; 2. qúnzhòng, A B C; 3. xuěqiāo, A B C;
4. xuǎncái, A B C; 5. quèxìn, A B C.

Unit 10
1. érsūn, A B C; 2. ěrxué, A B C; 3. èrzhàn, A B C;
4. ěrchuí, A B C; 5. èrxiàn, A B C.

Part Two: Reading exercises

1. Initials

1.1. b d g p t k

b — bāobàn, běibiān, búbiàn, bēnbō, bǎobèi, bìngbiàn, bīnbái, biāobǎng, bīngbàng, biǎobái

p — piānpō, pǐnpái, píngpàn, pǐpèi, pàpàng, péngpài, pǎopiān, pūpái, piáopō, pínpǔ

d — dǎidú, diūdiào, dǒudòng, diēdǎo, dàidòng, duōduān, dūndiǎn, dédàng, duìděng, duàndìng

t — tūntǔ, tāngtuán, tiáotíng, téngtòng, tiāntáng, tiětǎ, tàntīng, tóutāi, tuītuō, táotài

g — guòguān, gǎigé, guàguǒ, guǎigùn, gēnggǎi, guīgōng, gòugé, gāogēn, gǎnguāng, gànggǎn

k — kǔkǒu, kuàngkè, kāikěn, kùnkǔ, kuīkong, kuàngkēng, kuānkuò, kuākǒu, kànkāi, kěkào

1.2. z c s zh ch sh r

z — zāizāng, zìzé, zàngzú, zuòzéi, zìzūn, zǔzong, zuìzǎo, zèngzì, zǒuzuǐ, zàizuò

c — cāngcuì, cūcāo, cōngcù, cuòcí, cuīcù, cóngcǐ, céngcì, cāicè, cuǐcàn, cáncún

s — sèsù, sǎosao, sānsè, sōngsǎn, sùsuàn, sǔnsī, suísú, suǒsuì, sōusuǒ, sòngsāng

zh — zhànzhēng, zhǎngzhě, zhàozhái, zhūnzhūn, zhèngzhuàng, zhízhuó, zhuīzhú, zhōuzhuǎn, zhōngzhēn, zhuàizhù

ch — chángchéng, chāichuān, chēchuáng, chénchuī, chōngchì, chuōchuān, chōuchù, chūncháo, chuàichuáng, chǎnchú

sh — shǎnshuò, shāoshāng, shénshèng, shèshī, shàishāng, shuāngshù, shuǎishǒu, shéishuō, shōushi, shùnshuǐ

r — róuruǎn, rúruò, róurùn, róngrǔ, rěnràng, ráorén, rùnrì, ruǎnruò, rǎnrǎn, rùrè

1.3. j q x

j — jiāojuǎn, jiāngjūn, jiǎnjǔ, jūjìn, jiéjiāo, jiǎjiè, juéjìng, jiějué, jiǎngjiu, juǎnjìn

q — qiángquán, qúnqíng, qiǎngqiú, qiàqiǎo, qiūqiān, qièqǔ, quánqín, qiànquē, qiǎoqǔ, qiānqiú

x — xiǎoxié, xuānxiè, xíngxùn, xiǎoxuě, xiànxiàng, xiōngxiǎn, xióngxīn, xiūxián, xūxīn, xiàxué

2. Finals

2.1. a o e i -i1 -i2 u ü

a — dǎzá, pàdǎ, bāla, dǎchà, tāshā, hǎdá, pàzhā, bámá, dǎkǎ, gābā

o — bópó, mómo, pōmò, mòmò, mópò, bómó, pòwō, wǒmō, pòmò, mǒbó

e — zhéshè, kèchē, zéshé, hēde, tèkě, cèzhe, rèhé, chēzhé, kělè, gèsè

i — jítǐ, qìjī, xīqí, bítì, píqì, dǐqì, bǐxǐ, jīxī, qǐjí, xíjī

-i1 — zìcí, sīzì, cǐcì, zìsī, sìzì, cìsǐ, zìcǐ, sìcì, cìzì, sìzǐ

-i2 — rìshí, zhǐshǐ, rìzhì, zhìchǐ, shīshì, chīshí, zhīshi, chízhì, zhíchǐ, shīzhí

u — zhūrú, wúgù, zhǔfù, wǔrǔ, zhùsù, gùzhǔ, túfū, chūkù, tūchū, shūfu

ü — yújù, qūjū, yùjù, yǔxù, yúqū, qūyù, xūyú, qǔjù, xùyǔ, jǔyǔ

i & -i — jírì, xǐshì, tící, zǐxì, qìzhì, cìji, sījī, chídǐ, tīzi, sǐqī

-i1 & -i2 — shízì, zīzhì, cìrì, sìzhī, zìchí, cǐshí, zhìsǐ, rìzi, cízhí, shísì

u & ü — chūjú, xùzū, rùyù, jūzhù, shùjù, jǔchū, chǔxù, sūqū, xūdù, cùjū

2.2. ai ei ao ou an en ang eng ong

ai — pāimài, gàicài, hǎiwài, zāihài, shàitái, báimǎi, chāitái, dàimài, kāicǎi, zháikāi

ei — zéilèi, běifēi, shéilèi, mèimei, wèilěi, zhèibēi, gěishéi, lěilěi, pèibèi, děikēi

ao — shāobāo, cáocao, pāomáo, zāogāo, chǎosháo, zhàochāo, gāozhāo, kàoláo, ràodào, tǎoráo

ou — dōushòu, gǒutóu, chóumóu, kòuròu, zhōuyóu, dǒulou, chǒulòu, ròutou, zǒugǒu, còushǒu

an — zhǎnlǎn, bānlán, zàntàn, shānbǎn, cǎndàn, cānkàn, gǎnrǎn, pāntán, pánchan, zhǎnrán

en — běnrén, chènshēn, chénwěn, zhènfèn, rènshēn, gēnběn, pēnfèn, zhēnrén, fěnchén, céncén

ang — bāngmáng, cāngsāng, shàngkàng, rāngrang, fàngzhàng, gāngcháng, tàngshāng, gàngfáng, āngzāng, làngdang
eng — zhēngchéng, zēngshēng, shěngchéng, zhěngfēng, gēngshēng, kēngmēng, fēngzheng, shēngténg, péngsēng, cèngdèng
ong — cóngróng, kǒnglóng, gōngzhòng, róngdòng, zǒnggòng, tóngzōng, chōngdòng, tóngkǒng, lǒngtǒng, sòngzhōng

2.3. ia ie iao iu ian in iang ing iong
ia — yājià, xiàjiā, qiājià, jiāyā, jiājià, qiàqià, jiǎyá, xiàjià, yāxià, jiǎxiā
ie — xiéjiē, xiēxie, jiējiè, xiètiě, biéjie, qièqiè, jièdié, jiéyè, tiēqiè, xiēyè
iao — jiàotiáo, jiàoxiāo, biàojiāo, diàoqiáo, piāomiǎo, qiáoqiao, tiàojiǎo, xiǎodiào, tiáojiào, xiāoyáo
iu — qiújiù, diūqiú, niūniū, jiùyǒu, qiūyóu, jiǔliú, niúyóu, jiùqiú, yǒujiǔ, xiūjiù
ian — tiánbiān, diānxián, piānjiàn, qiǎnxiǎn, tiānqiàn, diànxiàn, jiānxiǎn, piànqián, biànqiān, jiǎnbiàn
in — jìnqīn, xīnqín, jìnxīn, qīnxìn, xīnjīn, jǐnjǐn, bīnlín, pīnyīn, jìnlín, pínmín
iang — liàngxiàng, xiāngjiāng, jiǎngxiàng, liángxiǎng, qiángxiàng, xiǎngliàng, qiāngxiǎng, xiāngxiàng, jiàngxiàng, niángniangqiāng
ing — bǐngxìng, qīngxǐng, bīngpíng, jīngbīng, jǐnglíng, bìngqíng, qīngtīng, dìngxíng, píngdìng, qíngjǐng
iong — xiōngyǒng, qióngxiōng, jiǒngjiǒng, xiōngqióng, jiǒngrán, kùnjiǒng, jiǒngkuàng, pínqióng, xiōngqiāng, xiàngxióng

2.4. ua uo uai ui uan un uang
ua — guàhuā, huāguā, shuǎshua, guàhuà, huàguā, zhuākòng, shuǎhún, kuàdǒu, zhuǎzi, huárùn
uo — kuòchuò, shuōguǒ, tuóluó, huǒguō, zhuózuò, luóguō, duōsuo, nuòruò, zuòcuò, zhuōhuò
uai — wàikuài, shuāihuài, zhuàihuài, chuǎicè, guàitāi, chuāizi, kuàizuǐ, guāiqiǎo, zhuàiduàn, kuàihuó
ui — zuìkuí, zhuīsuí, duìshuǐ, huíguī, zhuìhuǐ, shuǐkuí, cuīhuǐ, tuìshuì, huìchuī, zuìguì
uan — ruǎnduàn, guànchuān, kuǎnkuǎn, huànsuàn, luàncuàn, zhuǎnhuàn, shuānchuán, luànchuān, huánzuàn, tuántuánzhuàn
un — chūnsǔn, hùndùn, gǔncún, kùndùn, chūnkùn, wēncún, lùnwén, chúnzhēn, zhǔnbèi, túnkěn

uang — zhuàngkuàng, chuángkuàng, zhuānghuáng, kuàngchuáng, shuānghuáng, chuāngkuàng, zhuāngkuāng, shuāngkuàng, kuángwàng, guǎngkuò

2.5. üe üan ün

üe — lüèquē, xuěyuè, juéxué, quēxuè, yuèquē, quèyuè, yuēlüè, mièjué, nüèqiú, juékǒu

üan — quánjuàn, xuānyuán, quánxuǎn, yuánquān, xuǎnduàn, juǎnkuǎn, zhuànquān, quánguǎn, yuánxiān, juānxiàn

ün — jūnbèi, qúndǎo, xūnjué, jūnquǎn, qúnhūn, xúnqiú, jùnqiào, gǔxùn, jùnjié, duǎnqún

2.6. er

er1 — érgē, ěrbèi, érnǚ, ěrzhuì, zhōngěr, érxì, ěrgēn, cóngér, ěrhuán, yīnér

er2 — èrhūn, èrhuáng, èrnǎi, èrhuà, èrhu, èrxīn, èrliú, èrshěn, èrfù, èrlǎo

COMMON PROBLEMS IN PRONUNCIATION AND TONES

I. Pronunciation

1. Initials

1.1. b d g, p t k

The major problem concerning this group of initials comes from one's improper control of aspiration. Unlike in some Indo-European languages, in which the opposition between the set *b, d, g* and the set *p, t, k* lies in voicing, i.e. the former is voiced while the latter not, in Chinese the opposition between these two sets of sounds lies in aspiration: *b, d, g* are not aspirated, while *p, t, k* are aspirated (none of these initials is voiced). Since the opposition of aspiration does not exist in the mother tongue of some learners, they cannot make this distinction properly: some people cannot pronounce *p, t, k* with enough aspiration, so their intended *p, t, k* become *b, d, g;* and some people pronounce *b, d, g* with some aspiration, which results in *p, t, k*. Such mistakes, which lead to differences in meaning (*e.g.* '*wǒ bà*' is 'my father' and '*wǒ pà*' is 'I fear'), must be avoided. Compare: *bā pā, dā tā, gā kā.*

In pronouncing *d* and *t* the tip of the tongue should not be against the alveolar ridge, which causes too much friction, like **d *t*. The tip of the tongue should be against the upper teeth. Listen now to this distinction. (The sounds pronounced correctly will precede those pronounced incorrectly. This sequence of comparing different ways of pronouncing a sound or a tone will be followed in the whole discussion. In the written text incorrect sounds are indicated with an asterisk). Compare: *dā (*dā), tā (*tā), tī (*tī).*

When the initial *g* follows the final *ing/eng/ong*, some people pronounce it wrongly as [ŋ]. It should still be *g*. Compare: *zhōngguó (*zhōngguó), yīnggāi (*yīnggāi).*

1.2. z c s, zh ch sh r

A major problem concerning this group of initials relates to the position of the tip of the tongue. Whereas for *z, c* and *s* the tip is against the back of the upper teeth, for *zh, ch, sh* and *r* the tip curls up against the front part of the hard palate, and the tongue blade is low. Compared to the [dʒ] of 'jar', [tʃ] of 'church' and [ʃ] of 'sharp' in English, the Chinese *zh, ch* and *sh* are more posterior, and there is no lip-protrusion. Compare: *zá zhá* jar, *cè chè* church, *sà shà* sharp.

The distinction between aspirated and unaspirated sounds is also a problem for some people in pronouncing this group of initials. Whereas *c* and *ch* are aspirated, *z, s, zh, sh* and *r* are not. Compare: *cī, zī sī; chī, zhī shī rī.*

Another problem concerning *zh, ch* and *sh* is that some people mix them up with *j, q* and *x*. Although in each pair – *zh & j, ch & q, sh & x* – the two initials have some features in common, namely, the way of withholding the air flow in pronouncing them; they differ widely in terms of the tongue position: for *zh, ch, sh* the tip curls upward, and the tongue blade is pulled down; for *j, q, x* the tip curls downward, and the tongue blade is high up against the alveolar-palatal 'roof'. Compare: *zhī jī, chī qī, shī xī.*

The initial *r* should not be pronounced with lip-protrusion, nor lip-rounding (unless it precedes a final which requires lip-rounding). In other words, one's lips should be relaxed and not move when pronouncing it. The character *rén*, for instance, should not be pronounced as **ruén*, and *ròu* should not be pronounced as **ruòu*. Compared to the [ʒ] in English, *r* in Chinese is usually pronounced with less friction, and the tongue is more retracted. Compare: *rě*, measure, *rěn*, vision. For people who can pronounce well *zh, ch, sh,* but not *r*, they can achieve *r* easily by cutting the initial part of *zh, ch,* or *sh* while prolonging the latter part, like this: *zh~, r~, sh~, r~.*

1.3. j q x

The tongue positions in pronouncing these three initials are the same: with the tip against the root of the lower teeth, and the tongue blade against the alveolar-palatal 'roof'. The distinctions among them lie in the ways in which the air is released. *j* and *q* can be distinguished with aspiration: *q* is strongly aspirated, while *j* is not. Compare: *jià qià xià, jiè qiè xiè.*

ji should not be pronounced as **z+i*, nor **zh+i*. Compare: *jià (*zià *zhià), jiè (*ziè *zhiè).*

qi should not be pronounced as **c+i*, nor **ch+i*. Compare: *qià (*cià *chià), qiè (*ciè *chiè).*

xi should not be pronounced as **s+i*, nor **sh+i*. Compare: *xià (*sià *shià), xiè (*siè *shiè).*

1.4. m f n l h y w

These initials rarely cause problems. The initial *h* is pronounced with strong aspiration, *nǐ hǎo* 'how are you', for instance, should not be pronounced as **nǐ ǎo*, as some French speaking people sometimes tend to say. The opposition among the pronunciations of the letters 'h', 'ch' and 'g' in Dutch does not exist in Chinese, and *h* is usually pronounced with little friction, though this may vary in degree on different occasions and by different people.

2. Finals

2.1. a o e i -i u ü

2.1.1. a

When it is the only component of a final, *a* is a central vowel. It is neither the anterior [a], nor the posterior [ɑ], e.g. *ā, bā.* Nuances in pronouncing *a,* however, does not lead to difference in meaning. When *a* is one of the components of a compound final, it may become anterior, *e.g.* in '*an*' and '*ian*'; or posterior, *e.g.* in '*ao*' and '*ang*'. Compare: *má, mán, máo.*

2.1.2. o

Some people pronounce *o* wrongly as **o.* It should be *o,* which is pronounced with lip-rounding which turns from tight to loose, like a glide from *u* to *o*. This movement of the lips is important for the correct pronunciation. Compare: *wǒ* (**wǒ*), *pò* (**pò*).

2.1.3. e

The final *e* is difficult for many learners. It is a back vowel pronounced at the root of the tongue, and it is unrounded. There is no lip-protrusion. In contrast, the English, Dutch or French vowels which are close to the Chinese *e* are central or front vowels, and mostly rounded. Some people pronounce *e* wrongly with lip-protrusion or raise the tip of the tongue, and pronounce it as **e* or **er*. It should be *e*. Compare: *chē* (**chē*), *shè* (**shè*).

Some people pronounce *e* wrongly as a sound between *e* and *-i*. Compare: *chē* (**chē*), *shè* (**shè*).
Note that the letter 'e' as part of the finals *ie* or *üe* is not pronounced as *e*.

2.1.4. i and -i

The letter 'i' may stand, in *pinyin*, for the finals *i* and *-i*, which have complementary distribution: *-i* occurs only after *z, c, s, zh, ch, sh* or *r*, while *i* never does. In other words, except for the above mentioned cases, the letter 'i' is pronounced as *i* in *pinyin.*

'*i*'. The final *i* is not difficult to pronounce, yet one should know that *i* is usually pronounced with some friction, as *yi*, especially when there is no preceding initial. Compare: *yī*, **yī*.

'*-i*'. There are two subtypes of *-i*: (a) the *-i* which follows *z, c,* or *s* and (b) the *-i* which follows *zh, ch, sh* or *r*. In pronouncing the *-i* of the former set, the tip of the tongue is usually against the back of the upper teeth, while in pronouncing the *-i* of the latter set the tip is against the front part of the hard palatal. Some people curl their tongues too little in pronouncing the latter type of *-i*, which results in a sound between *e* and *-i*, like **-i*, thus *zhi* becomes **zhi*, which would make it difficult for the listener to tell whether the intended sound is *zhe* or *zhi*. Sometimes there are also people who curl their tongues too much for *zhi*, which results in **zhi*. Compare now the two sub-types of *-i*: *zī -i*(1), *zhī -i*(2), *-i*(1) *-i*(2), *zi zhi*.

Another common problem concerning *i* and *-i* is that some people mix up these finals due to the identical written form of these two sounds.

2.1.5. u and ü

The letter 'u' may stand for two finals: *u* and *ü*. *ü* is written without umlaut when it is preceded by the initial *j, q, x,* or *y*, which cannot precede the final *u*. It is only when *ü* is preceded by the initial *n* or *l*, which can precede both *u* and *ü*, the umlaut is written to make the distinction between them. In fact *ü* is more often found without umlaut, as there are more words with this sound after *j, q, x, y* than after *n* or *l*.

A common feature of these two finals is that they should be pronounced with lip-rounding, which is important for good pronunciation. A common problem is that some people mix up these finals due to their identical written form under the circumstances described above.

'*u*'. Some people pronounce *u* as a sound between *u* and *o*, as **u*, which is less posterior and with less lip-rounding. This can be improved by strengthening the lip-rounding and making it more posterior. It is pronounced as *u*. Compare: *mù* (**mù*), *zū* (**zū*), *chú* (**chú*).

'*ü*'. Some people often forget the lip-rounding, and pronounce *ü* as a sound between *ü* and *i*. It should be *ü*. Compare: *lǜ* (**lǜ*), *qù* (**qù*).

Although nuances in pronouncing *u* mentioned above do not lead to differences in meaning, a poorly pronounced *ü* may suggest *i* to the listener, which may cause misunderstanding.

Similar to *i*, which is pronounced as *yi* when there is no preceding initial, *ü* is pronounced as *yu*, when there is no preceding initial. Compare: yù **yù*.

2.2. ai ei ao ou an en ang eng ong

2.2.1. ai

The final *ai* is pronounced neither as the English letter 'i', for which the opening of the mouth is wider; nor as [ɛi], as the pronunciation convention in Dutch for the letters 'ei' suggests, for which the opening is narrower. It should be *ai*. Compare: *bài,* bite; *mái,* mei (in Dutch). Some people mispronounce it as **a-i*, which sounds like two finals. Compare: *ai* (**a-i*), *zài* (**zà-i*).

2.2.2. ei

The final *ei* should not be pronounced as [ɛi], as, for example the pronunciation convention in Dutch for the letters 'ei' suggests. It should be *ei*. Compare: *ei* (**ei*), *méi* (**méi*), *bèi* (**bèi*).

2.2.3. ao

The cause for the poor pronunciation of the final *ao* is often that the aperture is too narrow, and the *ao* is pronounced like [ɔu]. To avoid this, one should make the *a* sound in *ao* stronger. Compare: *māo* (**māo*), *nǐhǎo* (**nǐhǎo*).

2.2.4. ou

There are two common problems concerning this final: (1) Some people mispronounce it as [ɔu], which is too open for this final. Compare: *dōu,* (**dōu*)*, kòu,* (**kòu*). (2) Some people mix it up with *uo*, which is written with the same letters in an inverse order. Compare: *dōu duō, zǒu zuǒ.*

2.2.5. an

The 'a' in the final *an* is an anterior [a], and it is pronounced as [an]. It should not be pronounced as [ɑn], with a posterior [ɑ] in it. Compare: ā*n* (*ā*n*), *wǎnfàn* (**wǎnfàn*).

2.2.6. en

Some people pronounce *en* wrongly as [ɛn], like the combination of the letters 'e' and 'n' in "pen" in Dutch or in English. The final *en* starts from an *e* sound which is less posterior than the final *e*, and it is pronounced as [ən]. Compare: *rén* (**rén*)*, wèn* (**wèn*).

2.2.7. ang

The problem with this final is that some people cannot make a clear distinction between *an* and *ang*. The two nasal sounds in these finals are different: [n] is anterior, while [ŋ] is posterior. Compare: ā*ng ān, shàng shàn, pànwàng.*

2.2.8. eng

One of the problems with *eng* is similar to that with *en*, in that some people start this final with [ɛ], rather than with [ə]. It should be [əŋ], not [ɛŋ]. Compare: *néng (*néng), péngyou (*péngyou)*. Another problem with *eng* is similar to that with *ang*, in that some people cannot make the distinction between the two nasal sounds [n] and [ŋ]. Compare: *ēng ēn, hèng hèn, chéng chén.*

2.2.9. ong

The major problem with this final is that some people pronounce it without lip-rounding, as a mixture of *ang* and *eng*. This can be corrected by strengthening the lip-rounding, as required for the *u* sound, and pronounce it as *ong*. Compare: *ong (*ong), ong eng, yònggōng (*yònggōng)*.

2.3. ia iao ian iang ie iu in ing iong

2.3.1. Common features

The finals in this group are composed of *i* and another element which has been introduced in the preceding part. The second elements in these combinations are pronounced louder and longer than the first. This feature is also shared by the finals to be discussed in 2.4 and 2.5, which are compounds that begin with *u* or *ü*.The finals ***iao, iang,*** and ***iong*** are pronounced as the combinations of *i* and *ao, ang, ong*. People who have no problems with the components of these combinations usually have no problems with these finals.

2.3.2. ia

In *ia* the '*a*' can be pronounced as central [A] or anterior [a], which is less open than the '*a*' alone. Variations of the 'a' sound, however, do not lead to difference in meaning.

2.3.3. ian

The '*a*' in *ian* is pronounced neither as the anterior [a], as in *an*, nor as the posterior [ɑ], as in *ao*. The opening of the mouth is much narrower in this compound final, which is [iɛn]. Some people pronounce it wrongly as [ian] or [iɑn]. Compare: *ian (*ian, *ian), nián (*nián), xiàn (*xiàn)*.

2.3.4. ie

Some people cannot pronounce well the second part of this final, which is [ɛ], not [e]. In other words, this final is pronounced as [iɛ], not [ie]. Compare: *ie (*ie), xiè (*xiè), xiězì (*xiě zì)*.

2.3.5. iu

The final *iu* is the combination of the vowels *i* and *ou*, not that of *i* and *u*. But some people mispronounce it as the combination of *i* and *u*, as **iu*. Compare: *iu* (**iu*), *liù* (**liù*), *shíjiǔ* (**shíjiǔ*). In addition, *iu* should not be pronounced as [iɔu], which is too open. It should be [iou]. Compare: *iu* (**iu*), *jiǔ* (**jiǔ*), *diū* (**diū*).

2.3.6. in ing

The pronunciations of the combinations of the letters 'in' and 'ing' in English and in Dutch are similar to the Chinese finals *in* and *ing*, but not identical: in English and Dutch the vowel is [ɪ], whereas in Chinese it is [i]. Some people apply the pronunciation rules in English or in Dutch to pronounce the finals *in* and *ing*. Although this will not cause misunderstanding in meaning, it brings about a foreign accent. Compare: *in* (**in*), *ing* (**ing*), *mín* (**mín*), *tīng* (**tīng*).

Some people cannot make the distinction between *in* and *ing*. To pronounce *ing* correctly, one should combine *i* and [ŋ], not *in* and [ŋ]. In pronouncing *in* the tongue stretches to the front, while in pronouncing *ing* the tongue retracts. Compare: *in ing*, *qǐngjìn* (**qǐngjìn*).

2.4. ua uo uai ui uan un uang

2.4.1. Common features

The finals in this group are composed of *u* and another final. Their pronunciations are the combined pronunciations of the two. The most important point in the pronunciation of this group of finals is that just like *u*, all the finals in this group should be pronounced with lip-rounding. Except for *ui*, the problems concerning this group of finals have already been discussed previously.

2.4.2. ui

The final *ui* is the combination of *u* and *ei*, not *u* and *i*, and it should be pronounced as *ui*, not as **ui*. Compare: *ui* (**ui*), *duì* (**duì*). As is mentioned earlier, some people pronounce *ei* as [εi], and there are also people who pronounce *ui* as [uεi]. Compare: *ui* (**ui*), *guì* (**guì*), *huíjiā* (**huíjiā*). Some people pronounce *ui* without the lip-rounding for *u*, which results in a sound similar to *ei*. Compare: *duì* (**duì*), *zuì* (**zuì*).

2.5. üe üan ün

2.5.1. Common features

The finals in this group are composed of *ü* and another element. Like the finals of the *u* group, those of the *ü* group are also pronounced with lip-rounding, otherwise, *ü* would sound like a mixture of *ü* and *i*. Compare: *lüè* (**lüè*), *xuǎn* (**xuǎn*), *jūn* (**jūn*). Another problem is that some people mistake *ü* for *u*, which is mentioned in the discussion of *ü*.

2.5.2. üe

A problem with *üe*, which is similar to that with *ie*, is that some people cannot pronounce well the second element, which is [ɛ], not [e]. They mispronounce *üe* as [ye]. Compare: *ue* (**ue*), *xué* (**xué*), *jiějué* (**jiějué*).

2.5.3. üan

The *an* in *üan* may be pronounced, either as [an], just like the final *an*, or as [ɛn], like the *an* in *ian*, but not as [ɑn]. This compound final is pronounced as *üan*. Compare: *üan* (**üan*), *quàn* (**quàn*), *ānquán* (**ānquán*).

2.5.4. ün

There is usually no problem with *ün* if one has mastered *ü* and *en*.

2.6. er

There are two principal types of *er*, within which there are subtypes:

2.6.1. The final er

The *er* that is the final of a character. The final *er* cannot be preceded by any initial. There is a slight difference in pronunciation between the two subtypes of the final *er*:

(1) [ər], which starts from [ə], as the *er* in *ér* (zi) (son), we may call it '*er*1'.
(2) [ar], which starts from a sound similar to [a], as the *er* in *èr* (two), we may call it '*er*2'.

The difference between these two subtypes of *er* does not cause misunderstanding or ambiguity in meaning. Yet knowledge of this difference is helpful in achieving a better pronunciation. Compare *er*1 and *er*2: *ér, èr, ér* (**ér*), *èr* (**èr*), *èr érzi* (**èr érzi*).

2.6.2. The suffix er

The suffix *er* co-occurs with a character, as its suffix. In such cases the pronunciation of the character with *er* may be:

(1) the combination of the original sound of the character and *er*, in which *er* is added to the final (F+*er*). This is the case when *er* is added to the final *i*, *-i*, *ü*, *a*[1] (or *ia, ua*), *ie* or *üe*, e.g. *jī*, *jīr*, *zì*, *zìr*, *yú*, *yúr*, *bà*, *bàr*, *jué*, *juér*.

(2) the combination of the modified sound of the character and *er*, in which *er* is added to the final without its last part (F'+*er*). This is the case when *er* is added to *in, un, ün, en*, or *an*, and the 'n' in the final is dropped, e.g. *jīn*, *jīnr*, *dùn*, *dùnr*, *wán*, *wánr*; and when *er* is added to *ei*, *ui*, or *ai* (or *uai*), which becomes *e+er, u+er* or *a+er*, e.g. *bèi*, *bèir*, *duī*, *duīr*, *bái*, *báir*.

Note here that the pronunciations of *a, an* and *ai* with *er* are the same, as they all become *a+er*, e.g. *bà, bàr; bàn, bàr; bái, bár*. The same goes with *in+er* and *i+er*, as well as *ün+er* and *ü+er*. It is not so, however, in the case of *en/ei+er* and *e+er*, nor *un/ui+er* and *u+er*. Although when the ending of *en*[2], *ui* or *un* is dropped, it becomes *e* or *u*, the affixation of *er* to them is different from that to the final *e* or *u*: the pronunciation of the former is the combination of *e+er* or *u+er*, while that of the latter is not, which is discussed below. Compare now the adding of the suffix *er* to *gēn & gē*, and to *duì & dù*: *gēn, gēr, gē, gēr, gēr, gēr; duì, duìr, dù, dùr, duìr, dùr*.

(3) the initial plus the final which has been turned into a retroflex sound, in which the *e* sound of *er* is absent (rF). This is the case when *er* is added to *u, e, o, ao, uo, ou*, or *ng (ing, eng, ang, ong)*, e.g. *wū, wūr, gē, gēr, wō, wōr, máo, máor, míng, míngr, kòng, kòngr*.

To sum up these subtypes of suffix *er*, here is the outline:

(1) F+*er*: *i/-i/ü/a/ia/ua/ie/üe +er*,
(2) F'+*er*: *in/en/ün/un/an/ei/ui/ai +er*,
(3) rF: *u/e/o/ou/ao/uo/ng +er*.

Among these 3 subtypes the most difficult one for foreign learners is subtype 3, because one cannot pronounce a word with the suffix *er* by adding *er* sound to the final, as it is with the other two subtypes; and the retroflexion modifies the sound of the final, turning it into a sound unfamiliar to foreign learners. To pronounce well the suffix *er* with a final of the third subtype one should curl one's tongue to pronounce the final, rather than add *er* sound to the final.

II. Tones

1. First tone

There are two crucial points concerning the first tone: it has to be high in pitch and flat. Problems occur when one of those two is violated: (1) when the starting point within the speaker's register is too low, it results in a half third tone, compare: *ā ǎ, mā mǎ*; (2) when people cannot keep their voice stable, it results in a second tone, when the pitch goes up, or in a fourth tone, when the pitch goes down, compare: ā *á, ā à, mā má, mā mà.*

2. Second tone

The crucial point concerning the second tone is that it has to be rising. To make the rise possible, the starting point should not be high. Some people cannot make a rising tone, because they start from the high pitch of the first tone, and their voice cannot reach an even higher pitch. The result is that their intended second tone turns out to be, in fact, the first tone.

Some people have no problem when reading isolated characters with the second tone, but when they speak the rise in their second tone is insufficient, which makes the second tone sound like a half third tone. This can be corrected by lengthening the final, so that it can reach a higher point. For instance, people who say '*wǒ méi* (**měi*) *qù*' 'I did not go' can lengthen the syllable *méi* and say '*wǒ méi- qù*'.

3. Third tone

The third tone usually causes more problems than the other tones, because unlike the others it has three values: (1) the half third tone, which is a relatively flat low tone, and which is used when a third tone syllable is followed, without a pause, by a syllable of another tone[3], e.g. *hǎokàn*; (2) the full third tone, which is slightly falling and then rising, and which is used when a stressed syllable[4] is followed by a pause, e.g. *hǎo*; and (3) it may change to the second tone when followed by a third tone syllable, e.g. *nǐ* in '*nǐhǎo*' is said as '*níhǎo*', and '*yěhěnhǎo*' is '*yéhénhǎo*' or '*yěhénhǎo*'. Compare the three types of the third tone: *hǎochī, hǎo, hǎomǎi.*

The major problem with regard to the third tone is the 'half third tone', which is more frequently used than the full third tone, because a syllable is more often followed by another syllable than by a pause. Some learners are so used to its full contour that they simply cannot cut its rising end and turn it into the half third tone. The result is that their intended third tone sounds like the second tone. For example, instead of saying *měiguó*, some say **méiguó.*

Occasionally there were also learners who failed to use the full contour when it should be used, e.g. in response to a question with '*hǎoma*' 'is it good...' one should use the full contour of the third tone, not the half third tone, to say '*hǎo*', which is followed by a pause.

For many learners the most difficult tone combination pattern is a third tone followed by a second tone (3&2). In anticipation of the rising tone which follows the third tone, they cannot help raising the half third tone, which should be low. For example, some people pronounce *yǔyán* as **yúyán*. Some learners find it even more difficult to keep the half third tone low when it is followed by a neutral tone, e.g. *wǎnle*. They use a second tone instead, as **wánle*.

Another problem with the third tone is related to its change into the second tone. When there are two consecutive third tone syllables, the last one retains the third tone, while the preceding one usually changes into the second tone. However, some learners retain the third tone of the preceding syllable, and change the following one into the second tone. For example, they say *hěnhǎo* as **hěnháo* and *yěyǒu* as **yěyóu*.

In a string of three or more consecutive third tone syllables, the tone pattern of the last two syllables usually abides by the rules described above, and the preceding syllable(s) usually can be either the third tone or the second tone, if they are mono-syllabic words, e.g. in the sentence '*wǒ yě hěn hǎo*' 'I am also fine', in which all the syllables have the third tone, the first two syllables can be 2&3, 2&2 or 3&2, while the last two syllables are 2&3.

When a third tone syllable which is not the last one in a string is the last syllable of a word of two (or more) third tone syllables, e.g. '*wǔ*' in the sentence '*Lǐwǔ yě hěn hǎo*' 'Liwu is also fine', in which *wǔ* is not the last syllable of this third tone string, but is the last syllable of a word composed of two third tone syllables, *wǔ* cannot be changed into the second tone if the preceding syllable, which is '*Lǐ*' in this sentence, retains the third tone. One should not say '**Lǐwú yé hén hǎo*' (***32** 2 2 3). It should be '*Líwǔ yé hén hǎo*' (**23** 2 2 3) or '*Líwú yě hén hǎo*' (**22** 3 2 3). In other words, when a word of two (or more) third tone syllables precedes a third tone syllable, the last syllable of this word can change into the second tone only if the preceding syllable also changes into the second tone.

Even in a sentence with three third tone syllables such as '*tā liǎojiě wǒ*' '(s)he knows me well' (in which the tone pattern of the sentence is 1 **33** 3), though *jiě* immediately precedes the last syllable in this string of third tone syllables, it cannot be changed into the second tone if *liǎo* retains the third tone. We cannot say '**tā liǎojié wǒ*' (*1 **32** 3). We say '*tā liáojiě wǒ*' (1 **23** 3) or '*tā liáojié wǒ*' (1 **22** 3).

4. Fourth tone

The crucial point concerning the fourth tone is that it has to be falling. To make the fall possible, the starting point should not be low. People who start the fourth tone from a low point will be unable to drop the pitch, and their intended fourth tone will result in a half third tone.

Similar to the problem with the second tone, in which the rise (or the pitch range) is insufficient, a problem with the fourth tone is that the fall of the pitch is insufficient, which makes the fourth tone sound like a first tone. This can also be corrected by lengthening the final, which will enable the falling pitch to reach a lower point.

5. Neutral tone

The neutral tone is used for modal particles, which are almost always unstressed, or for characters which have other tones and which are used in unstressed syllables, in which their original tones are lost. The pitch of a syllable with the neutral tone is usually lower than that of the original tone, except when the original tone is the third tone, which is already at the bottom of one's register. Compare the tones in the following words in which the first syllables have the original tones and the second syllables have the neutral tone: *māma, yéye, nǎinai, bàba.* The tone of the preceding syllable and the intonation of the sentence may also affect the pitch of the neutral tone.

6. Problems of tones in a string of syllables

Some learners have no problem with tones when pronouncing individual characters, but they have problems with tones in a string of syllables. There are often problems in the following cases: (1) when a syllable of the third tone is followed by another syllable, they cannot keep the half third tone low; (2) when two or more consecutive syllables have the same tone, they use different tones; (3) when a syllable of the falling tone is followed by a syllable of the rising tone, or vice versa, the fall or rise is insufficient. A major cause for the third problem is that the pronunciation of the tone of the preceding syllable is affected by the anticipation of the tone of the following syllable, e.g. instead of saying *dìtú,* some people say *dītú.* The anticipation of the rising tone of *tú* prevents the drop of *dì.* To avoid this kind of mistake, one may try to pause after saying the first syllable.

APPENDIX

I. Rules to remember

1. Aspiration

Aspirated: p/t/k/c/ch/q;
Unaspirated: b/d/g/z/zh/j.

2. i vs -i

-i: after z/c/s/zh/ch/sh/r;
i: except for the above mentioned circumstances.

3. u vs ü

ü: with two dots on the top after *n* or *l*, or without the two dots after j/q/x/y;
u: except for the above mentioned circumstances.

4. iu and ui

iu: *iu* is in fact *i* + *ou*, not *i* + *u*;
ui: *ui* is in fact *u* + *ei*, not *u* + *i*.

5. Ways in which the letter 'a' is pronounced in different finals:

[A]: a, ua, ia   [a]: ai, an, uai, uan
[ɛ]: ian, üan   [ɑ]: ao, ang, uang, iao, iang

6. Ways in which the letter 'e' is pronounced in different finals:

[ɤ]: e   [ə]: en, eng, er
[e]: ei   [ɛ]: ie, üe

7. Third tone

7.1. Full contour vs half contour

Full contour: when a stressed third tone syllable is followed by a pause;
Half contour: when a third tone syllable is followed by a syllable of another tone.

7.2. Change to the second tone

(1) 33 or 3 3 (the space between two '3's implies that the two syllables do not belong to the same word) usually becomes 23 or 2 3.
(2) 33 3 may change to 22 3 or 23 3, but not 32 3.

II. Key to the Listening Exercises (Set I) (list of words which are read correctly)

Unit 1

(A)

1. fā, A; 2. mì, B; 3. hǎo, A C; 4. lí, A B; 5. nào, C.

(B)

1. fā, A; 2. mì, B C; 3. hǎo, B; 4. lí, B C; 5. nào, B.

Unit 2

(A)

1. yū, A; 2. yē, A B; 3. wō, C; 4. wū, B; 5. hē, A;
6. fēn, A; 7. niē, B; 8. mó, A; 9. lǚ, A C; 10. mèn, B.

(B)

1. yū, A; 2. yē, B C; 3. wō, C; 4. wū, B; 5. hē, B;
6. fēn, A B; 7. niē, B; 8. mó, A C; 9. lǚ, B C; 10. mèn, B.

Unit 3

(A)

1. bó, A; 2. pén, B C; 3. dié, B C; 4. tú, B; 5. ké, A;
6. píbāo, B; 7. géhé, A C; 8. táopǎo, C; 9. túdì, B C; 10. pípa, B.

(B)

1. bó, A C; 2. pén, C; 3. dié, A; 4. tú, C; 5. ké, A C;
6. píbāo, A; 7. géhé, C; 8. táopǎo, A C; 9. túdì, C; 10. pípa, A.

Unit 4

(A)

1. sǐ, A; 2. cǐ, B C; 3. shǐ, A; 4. zhǐ, C; 5. chǐ, B C;
6. zǐsè, C; 7. shǐshū, C; 8. dǐzhì, A B; 9. zhǐzé, B; 10. rìzi, A C.

(B)

1. sǐ, A C; 2. cǐ, A; 3. shǐ, C; 4. zhǐ, A; 5. chǐ, B;
6. zǐsè, C; 7. shǐshū, C; 8. dǐzhì, A; 9. zhǐzé, C; 10. rìzi, C.

Unit 5

(A)

1. zǒu, B C; 2. pěng, A C; 3. dǎn, A C; 4. tǎng, B C; 5. hǎigǎng, C;
6. shěngwěi, B; 7. chǎngzhǎng, A; 8. zǒngtǒng, C; 9. lǎobǎn, B; 10. shǐzhě, C.

(B)

1. zǒu, A C; 2. pěng, C; 3. dǎn, B; 4. tǎng, A B; 5. hǎigǎng, B C;
6. shěngwěi, C; 7. chǎngzhǎng, A B; 8. zǒngtǒng, B; 9. lǎobǎn, C;
10. shǐzhě, A.

Unit 6

(A)

1. xù, A B; 2. jì, C; 3. qìn, B C; 4. xìn, B; 5. jìnqū, C;
6. xìngqu, A; 7. qíngxù, A; 8. qìngxìng, C; 9. jùjí, B; 10. jīqì, B.

(B)

1. xù, A; 2. jì, C; 3. qìn, A C; 4. xìn, C; 5. jìnqū, B C;
6. xìngqu, C; 7. qíngxù, C; 8. qìngxìng, C; 9. jùjí, A; 10. jīqì, C.

Unit 7

(A)

1. jiā, B C; 2. qiǎo, B C; 3. qióng, C; 4. xiù, C; 5. xiōngqiāng, A;
6. jiēqià, B; 7. xiàqu, B; 8. xiānliang, C; 9. xiōngdi, A; 10. jiùying, B.

(B)

1. jiā, A; 2. qiǎo, A B; 3. qióng, B; 4. xiù, C; 5. xiōngqiāng, C;
6. jiēqià, A C; 7. xiàqu, B; 8. xiānliang, C; 9. xiōngdi, A; 10. jiùying, C.

Unit 8

(A)

1. zhuā, A C; 2. zuò, B; 3. guǎi, A B; 4. kuí, C; 5. huánghūn, A;
6. zuǒyòu, B C; 7. zuìkuài, C; 8. guóhuà, C; 9. cúnkuǎn, B C;
10. guòguān, C.

(B)

1. zhuā, A; 2. zuò, B; 3. guǎi, A; 4. kuí, B; 5. huánghūn, B;
6. zuǒyòu, B; 7. zuìkuài, C; 8. guóhuà, A B; 9. cúnkuǎn, B;
10. guòguān, C.

Unit 9

(A)

1. qún, A B; 2. xuān, B C; 3. xuè, A; 4. juǎn, A C; 5. chǔxù, B;
6. chuánxùn, B; 7. quánsù, B C; 8. zūnxún, C; 9. quèqiè, B; 10. quēxiàn, B.

(B)

1. qún, B; 2. xuān, C; 3. xuè, A; 4. juǎn, B C; 5. chǔxù, B;
6. chuánxùn, B; 7. quánsù, B; 8. zūnxún, B C; 9. quèqiè, C; 10. quēxiàn, B.

Unit 10

(A)

1. érqiě, A; 2. èrbǎi, A C; 3. ěrduo, B; 4. shíèr, C; 5. yīng'ér B C.

(B)

1. érqiě, B C; 2. èrbǎi, C; 3. ěrduo, C; 4. shíèr, A C; 5. yīng'ér A.

III. Key to the Listening Exercises (Set III) (list of words which are read correctly)

Unit 1
1. māomī, B C; 2. máofà, A; 3. fāmá, A C; 4. hǎola, A; 5. lìfǎ, C.

Unit 2
1. yèli, B; 2. wūmiè, A; 3. móhé, C; 4. yùmèn, A; 5. wǒè, B.

Unit 3
1. tiěké, A; 2. bēnbō, B; 3. pǎobù, 0; 4. dàgē, C; 5. gūpì, B.

Unit 4
1. sìchǐ, 0; 2. zīshì, A; 3. cǐzhì, B; 4. zhírì, A; 5. chìzì, B.

Unit 5
1. kǒubēi, B; 2. chéngzhǎng, 0; 3. zàntóng, C; 4. shèngcài, B; 5. zhōngbān, C.

Unit 6
1. jīzhì, A; 2. cíqì, C; 3. xǐshì, B; 4. jìngxīn, C; 5. qīnqíng, A.

Unit 7
1. jiāojiē, A; 2. qiānqiǎng, A; 3. jǐujiā, 0; 4. xióngxìng, B; 5. qiǎngxiǎn, B.

Unit 8
1. zhuāngsuàn, B; 2. zuǐchún, 0; 3. huāhuán, A C; 4. guàizuì, 0; 5. cúnhuó, A.

Unit 9
1. juānkuǎn, A; 2. qúnzhòng, C; 3. xuěqiāo, C; 4. xuǎncái, B; 5. quèxìn, A.

Unit 10
1. érsūn, A C; 2. ěrxué, A; 3. èrzhàn, A; 4. ěrchuí, C; 5. èrxiàn, B.

NOTES

1 In this text the pronunciation of the suffix *er* is presented in two ways: (1) add [ər] sound to the final, and (2) pronounce the final with curling tongue, which turns the final into a retroflex sound, in which the [ə] sound of *er* is absent. In fact, however, there are various grades of audibility of the [ə] sound in the affixation of *er*, and the division between these two types is not a clear-cut dichotomy as is presented here. It is for the convenience of learning/teaching that the pronunciation of suffix *er* is presented like this. The affixation of *er* to the final *a* lies, for example, between the two principal types, but it is categorized in this book as belonging to the first type.

2 The affixation of *er* to *en, ei* or *-i* may also be treated as a separate subtype, in which the complete final, rather than just the ending 'n' or 'i', is dropped, and the pronunciation is the combination of the initial and [ər], e.g. *yìběn+er, mōhēi+er, táicí+er.*

3 When a third tone syllable is followed by a syllable of the neutral tone whose original tone is also the third tone, the former usually has the half third tone, e.g. *jiějiě* is pronounced as *jiějie*, not as **jiéjie*, and *yǐzǐ* as *yǐzi,* not *yízi.* The tone sandhi of *xiǎojiě* is an exception, which should be *xiáojie*, not *xiǎojie.*

4 When a third tone syllable before the pause is unstressed, usually it is also the half third tone, rather than the full contour of the third tone, which is used, e.g. in sentences *yǒurén* ***zhǎo*** *nǐ* 'someone is **looking for** you' and *tā* ***rènshi*** *wǒ*, 'he **knows** me', the half third tone is used for *nǐ* and *wǒ.* We do not say **yǒurén zhǎo* ***nǐ*** *or *tā rènshi* ***wǒ***, unless these words are stressed as contrasting elements (as against other people).

REFERENCES

Chen, Mingyuan et al. 1983. *Rudiments of Chinese Phonetics*. Beijing: Foreign Language Press.

DeFrancis, John. 1976. *Beginning Chinese*. New Haven and London: Yale University Press.

Huang, Raymond. 1981. *Mandarin Pronunciation*. Hongkong: Hong Kong University Press.

Liu, Xun et al. 2009. *New Practical Chinese Reader I*. Beijing: Beijing Language and Culture University Press.

PRINTED ON PERMANENT PAPER • IMPRIME SUR PAPIER PERMANENT • GEDRUKT OP DUURZAAM PAPIER - ISO 9706

N.V. PEETERS S.A., WAROTSTRAAT 50, B-3020 HERENT